Seasons and Senses
Copyright © 2022 by Darlene T. Ewers

All rights reserved. No part of this book may be reproduced or transmitted in any form or by any means, electronic or mechanical, including photocopying, recording, or by any information storage and retrieval system without express written permission from the author, except in the case of brief quotations embodied in critical reviews and certain other noncommercial uses permitted by copyright law.

Printed in the United States of America.

Brilliant Books Literary
137 Forest Park Lane Thomasville
North Carolina 27360 USA

SEASONS

AND

SENSES

POETRY & OTHER THOUGHTS

BY DARLENE T. EWERS

TABLE OF CONTENTS

CHAPTER 1 – SPRING   7

    A BRAND NEW DAY   9
    FIRE   11
    GOD'S TEARS   13
    HOPE   15
    MAMA'S SWEATER   17
    PROMISES   19
    SUNSHINE   21
    THE LITTLE GIRL   23
    VIOLET DAYS   25
    WE THREE   27

CHAPTER 2 – SUMMER   29

    DIAMONDS   31
    GRAINS OF SAND   33
    HANDS   35
    MEMORIES   37
    ON BECOMING A MAN   39
    THE FLAG   41
    THE PATRIOT   43
    THE PELICAN   45
    THE SEA   47
    THREE SISTERS   49

CHAPTER 3 – AUTUMN   53

    AUTUMN LEAVES   55
    EMOTIONS   57
    MY GUARDIAN ANGEL   59
    SUNFLOWERS   61
    THANKFULNESS   63
    THANKSGIVING DAY REMEMBERED   65
    THE HARP   67
    THE SWEATER   69
    THE TRINITY   73
    THE WINDOW OF MY WORLD   75

CHAPTER 4 – WINTER   77

    CHRISTMAS MEMORIES   79
    GRACE   81
    GRANDMA'S SUGAR COOKIES   83
    SEASONS AND SENSES   87
    SISTERS   89
    THE GIVING TREE   91
    THE THREE LITTLE GIRLS   93
    TIME   95
    WINTER WONDERLAND   97

DEDICATION

To James Byron Ewers
in honor of our golden wedding anniversary,
June 29, 1968 - 2018.

SPRING

CHAPTER 1

BY DARLENE T. EWERS

A Brand New Day

Early on a Sunday morn, many years ago,
The sole Redeemer rose from death to greet the glorious day.

No one saw Him come to life, only men divine.
The power was given to Him by God to conquer Satan's plan.

The young maiden knew God's will. The Son came through her.
His human father taught Him well, as did His Father, God.

He taught the Temple rulers, wise and fine was He.
They pondered what He said to them and stored it deep inside.

As He walked across the land, many saw His deeds.
They sang His praises endlessly, but harbored evil thoughts.

He healed the sick with godly power, calling forth the dead.
The humble bowed before His feet and kissed His gentle hands.

Spreading robes upon the ground, calling Him the LORD,
Hallelujahs and palms were raised, while traitors planned His death.

Late one night, He sorrowed much, praying for relief.
The blood was pouring from His brow as he trembled on His knees.

His disciples fell asleep, lying down to rest.
He asked them to keep watch one hour, while He alone would pray.

Night's dark hour was sadly spent while He lingered there.
The agents that arrived that night were demons in disguise.

The traitor came face to face with the Holy Son.
"Whom do you seek tonight, my friend?"
"My Master and my friend!"

With the kiss, the die was cast: it was Satan's plan.
Throughout the night and dreaded day, they beat and spat on Him.

The scourging whip beat His back, tearing skin and flesh.
A crown of thorns was placed upon His head with brutal force.

Jeering, laughing in His face, they displayed His form.
"Crucify Him", they quickly said, "and let the murderer go."

The shouting crowd swore at Him as the guards tied His wrists.
They placed upon His shoulders bare a heavy wooden cross.

To the Mount of Golgatha He carried forth His load.
The friends had left, but many saw Him carry on in woe.

The gleeful crowd cheered Him on as He carried now His cross.
Beside the path, the women stood, observing all that was.

They stripped Him bare, greedily betting for His robe.
Once laid upon the heavy wood, they drove the nails through.

His hands and feet trembled then as searing, shocking pain
Ran through His outstretched arms and legs.
Call now upon Your God!"

For three hours He lingered there, speaking seven times.
By His will, He gave up His life, bowed down His head, and died.

Late that night, His friends returned, taking down His form.
A special man had given his own tomb to bury now the dead.

The women wrapped Him quickly, sprinkling on the spice.
They placed Him in the borrowed tomb, and sealed it for the night.

Early on the Easter morn, women came again
To finalize His burial bed, and saw the stone removed.

Looking deep within the cave, angels spoke to them:
"Fear not, He's not here, but alive! Go tell His friends He lives!"

"Sir, where have you taken Him?" -- "It is I!", He said.
"Go, tell my friends to go ahead and meet in Galilee."

The Son of God who arose from death now greets each Easter morn!

SPRING October 31, 2017

FIRE

Temper, temper, little fire!
Bursting forth it glows with ire.
Raging onward, turning black,
I know that now we can't hold back.

Feelings mutual, tempers flare!
They die down and retreat to lair.
Oh, dear God, why must we fight,
As day turns into the black of night?

Sorrow fills the void now kept
Deep within our souls' dark pit.
If each of us only knew the love
That now lies dormant — as said above.

Gentle Spirit, tender dove,
Fill us now with Your sweet love.
Help us reclaim the time that's lost
As a promise each one treasures most.

May our love for one another
Help us not the Spirit smother,
But lift us up and help us reclaim
The Father, Son, and Spirit's Name!

GOD'S TEARS

Peering through the gossamer film of the curtains at my sash,
I see the dripping eaves and hear the drops that splash.

Is God weeping for me and all the sins of man?

Crying at the prospects for my distant friends, or foe,
I cannot help but wonder how God must love us so.

Did Christ weep for me when on the cross He died?

Remembering each, and everyone, He didn't sin like me,
But He died for those who caused Him so much grief.

Do I think of His betrayal by sinful man and me?

On rainy days, I look beyond the darkened sky
And listen to the sighs of God in each, and every cloud.

How much longer will He wait for us to change?

God gives us life and breathe to take us through each day,
But we forget to thank Him and only just complain.

What does He do all day while we go groaning by?

He gives us faith to live within His daily plan,
But we think we know much more than He and labor in our pain.

When will God give up on us and ask us to explain?

He gives us hope each day when we call upon His name,
But then we soon forget to thank Him once again.

Where is hope to be found when we forget His name?

He gives us love through Christ, who died and lives again.
Despite all we've done, He calls us home to Him.

Who will live today to sin again, and die eternally?

God gives us grace through His Spirit, who lives inside our hearts.
Will we open up once more, and allow Him to come in?

I choose to live in grace today, and claim my victory!

HOPE

When the snowy wind blows
    Its cold breath from the North,
I long in my heart
    For spring's merry lark.

The stars in the sky
    And the moon's soft glow
Give hope for the dawn
    Of morning's new day.

The rosy sun rises
    On new fallen snow
Giving promise of life
    To spring's afterglow.

The birds sing their praise
    To our Father on high
Heralding the start
    Of a bright new day.

Mama's Sweater

When I was just a sprout, running all about,
Mama wore her sweater, inside the house and out.
It kept her warm and cozy from winter into spring;
She never wore it out!

I do not know when or how she got it;
Perhaps it was a gift or a hard-earned reward.
But throughout those simple times on the farm,
Her sweater kept her warm!

I forgot that soft, old sweater until she had died.
While going through her household things, I came upon the past.
The sweater brought me memories,
And I wanted them to last!

The sweater is a soft reminder of simpler days
While growing up and living on the farm.
While feeding the chickens or collecting their eggs,
She always wore the sweater!

The faded sweater is a simple reminder
of long gone days and lingering memories.
While sitting in my chair, or snuggling on the couch,
My sweater warms me in and out!

Mama has left her toil behind,
But her sweater reminds me of gentler days.
I hope that when I lay her sweater down,
Someone will claim their own lost times!

PROMISES

The sleeping child in yonder room
Bequeaths upon us her tender love.
Little eyes so pure and bright
Do not cloud when I come into sight.

Pillow cheeks and button nose,
And lips of rosy cupid bows
Beckon to us every morn:
This new day she will sweetly adorn.

Tender cries will ask for love
As squeals of laughter soar above
Tinkling down upon our ears:
Ringing through the distant years.

Oh, but that this gentle love
Would always remain so true:
Soft and tender, trusting, too,
Not encumbered, or ever blue.

She promises always to remain
My gentle grandchild without shame.
Sweet and gentle, loving, too,
Loyal forever until the end!

SUNSHINE

Sunshine comes in varied forms:
The light of dawn,
My child's bright eyes,
Dewdrops on roses, and
A smile on your face.

It comes to us unearned:
The new day's dawn,
My grandchild's eyes,
Unplanned roses, and
My loved one's face.

Sonshine comes in God's own Son:
The Easter dawn,
My Savior's eyes,
Thorns on roses and
My Savior's face.

He comes to warm my soul:
To banish Satan,
To conquer sins,
To remove all death, and
Welcome me with His smiling face.

The Little Girl

With ponytails flying, she runs across the lawn:
Bob, bob, bobbing along.
Turning to smile, she greets the new dawn!
Smile, smile, smiling away!

While the years fly by, she greets each new day:
Laugh, laugh, laughing aloud.
Reading, and writing, and summing away:
Dream, dream, dreaming today!

Grade school and high school and college glide by:
Study, study, studying each day.
"Time stands still for no one", they say:
Sleep, sleep, sleeping – no way!

Today we celebrate the goals she's reached:
Hurray, hurray, hooraying for her!
The diploma is real – she made the grade!
Graduate, graduate, graduating today!

And now her hands reach out:
Help, help, helping the sick!
May the Great Physician guide all her days:
Heal, heal, healing always!

Into His hands we bid you Godspeed:
Pray, pray, praying each day!!
His Spirit will comfort and lead you – take heed:
Listen, listen, listening – today!

SPRING May 18, 2008

VIOLET DAYS

SPRING HAS COME UPON US NOW;
IT BECKONS TO EMERALD GRASSY MOW.
PEEKING O'ER THE STILTED SPIKES,
TIPTOE NOW YOU TINY CAPS!

OH, HOW OFT' YOUR TENDER HUE
HAS BECKONED UNTO ME.
BIDDING COME AND PICK ME NOW
TO BESTOW UPON A TENDER BROW.

MORNING LIGHT DOES QUICKLY POSE
DEWDROPS SWEET UPON MY NOSE.
QUICKLY NOW, DEPART TODAY;
COME AGAIN, ANOTHER DAY.

WE THREE

The smile on Mama's round face
And the gleam in Daddy's blue eyes
Were but a foretaste of what we would be.

As the years roll by so regularly
We can't help but see how much we are
A pattern of she and he.

When I consider the second one's eyes,
With bright blue skies and sweeping lash,
It's Daddy's that I see.

When I consider the third child's eyes,
With grassland's green and shaded tree,
It's Mama's that I see.

And whose hair does she own?
The long blonde flax
Or auburn tress?

Or the hands and feet?
Are they our mother's hands?
And our father's feet?

And yet, as much unalike as we are,
We share a commonality –
For in each of these – I see me!

Our love began with them
And continues today –
To nurture us – we three!

SUMMER

CHAPTER 2

BY DARLENE T. EWERS

DIAMONDS

After yesterday's rain washed my dappled pines,
The morning sunshine revealed tiny raindrops
Like so many sparkling diamonds.

Refreshed by hearty spring showers,
Each towering spire restored my hopes
While viewing creation's waking moments.

Although my rising hour aroused my pains,
They subsided during the time it takes
To reflect on today's new promises.

Just as God set His promise at rainbows' ends, So,
too, He gives me sparkling diamonds
To strengthen my faith for tomorrow's times.

Grains of Sand

Humans are as unique as the grains of sand on the seashore.
Molded and shaped by the friction of time,
They evolve into unique particles.

One is turned this way, the other that, by the rolling waves of life;
And as they glide onto the shore of life,
They exhibit their true essence.

A combination of similar substance, yet each one remains unalike.
Each molecule contributes to the diversity
And the outcome is stunning.

I wish we were more alike, but then our world would be sterile.
Every individual contributes
To the overall beauty of man.

How similar we humans are in all our attributes.
How unfamiliar we become as we age.
Life makes its marks on each.

Our beginning is common among men,
But our lives make us what we are,
And separately we are unalike.

I cannot change one grain of sand on the shore,
Nor can I dictate that of another.
Even my siblings aren't like me.

We used to be one family of man,
But now we are divided by time
And I am all alone in life.

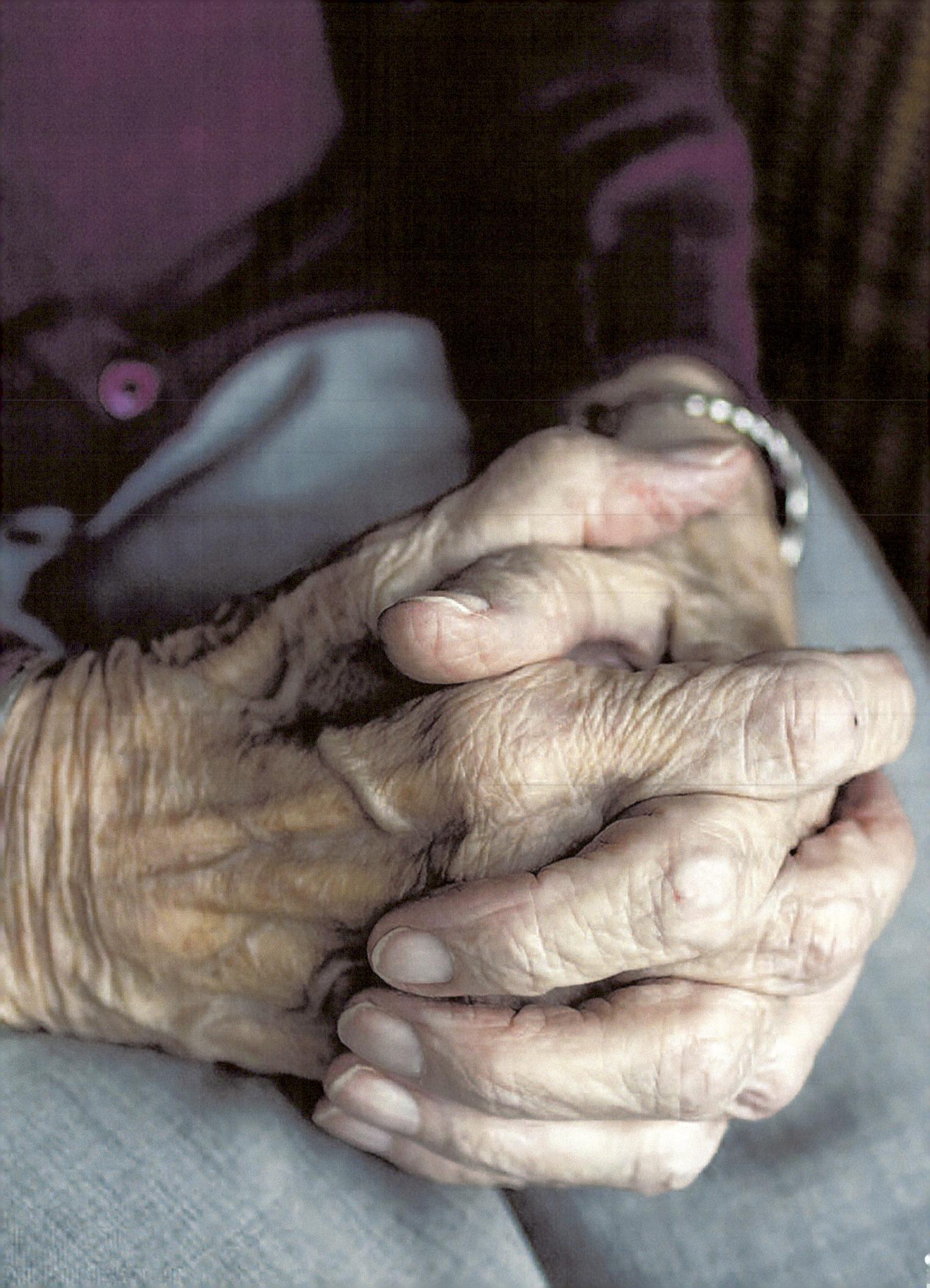

HANDS

What is it about hands that are so intriguing?
We all come equipped with an adequate pair.
But when holding a new child, the first thing I admire
Are the delicate layers of thin paper nails
With small crescent moons at their edges.

The orbs of fingers and toes is then what I see.
Those plump round hands with protruding digits
Don't compare to the stars in the heavens.
They grasp my fingers, connecting with their mother.
They grab my heart's strings immediately.

As those delicate instruments reach out to explore,
They encounter the world all around.
They grab onto hair, ears, toes, and even their nose
hen reaching out, touch ours.
It's another human reaching out to me.

Crawling and reaching up to stand,
The exploration continues for years beyond.
The silkiness of water and subtle texture of sand
Are all a part of learning about the world,
Attempting to comprehend it all.

By the time their school years come into view,
Those little hands have experienced many a clue.
Teaching them to form letters and shapes is exciting
And only the beginning of entering a new phase:
That of learning their numbers and words.

They learn to play games with all their friends.
They learn to dry dishes and pick up their toys.
The little one graduates to bigger and better tasks.
Opening the world to what it means to help another
And to be a contributing citizen.

At the end of their grades, they make commitments
To their graduation efforts, to God and country, and
Saluting the flag, pledging allegiance
To powers that be and to one another.
Some of them choose to tend their own little garden.

When the next generation appears on the scene,
Helping hands take care of their little ones.
The scene is repeated once again for a generation
When the cycle repeats to help others;
And lifting them, they lift one another.

As generation after generation follows,
We see the aging hands doing their tasks.
I loved to watch my grandmother's hands
Peeling potatoes or making homemade bread.
She offered a reward for quietly watching.

Those hands once changed her children's clothes,
Wiped tears from crying eyes and tended wounded knees.
They made cookies and bread, cakes and pies,
And welcomed visitors with a hearty cup of brew,
While making more meals than could be counted.

When I met my husband's grandfather,
The greatest compliment I ever was given
Was when he said my hands reminded him of his wife's.
She was a wife, mother, cook, and believer,
I see the Bible resting in her hands.

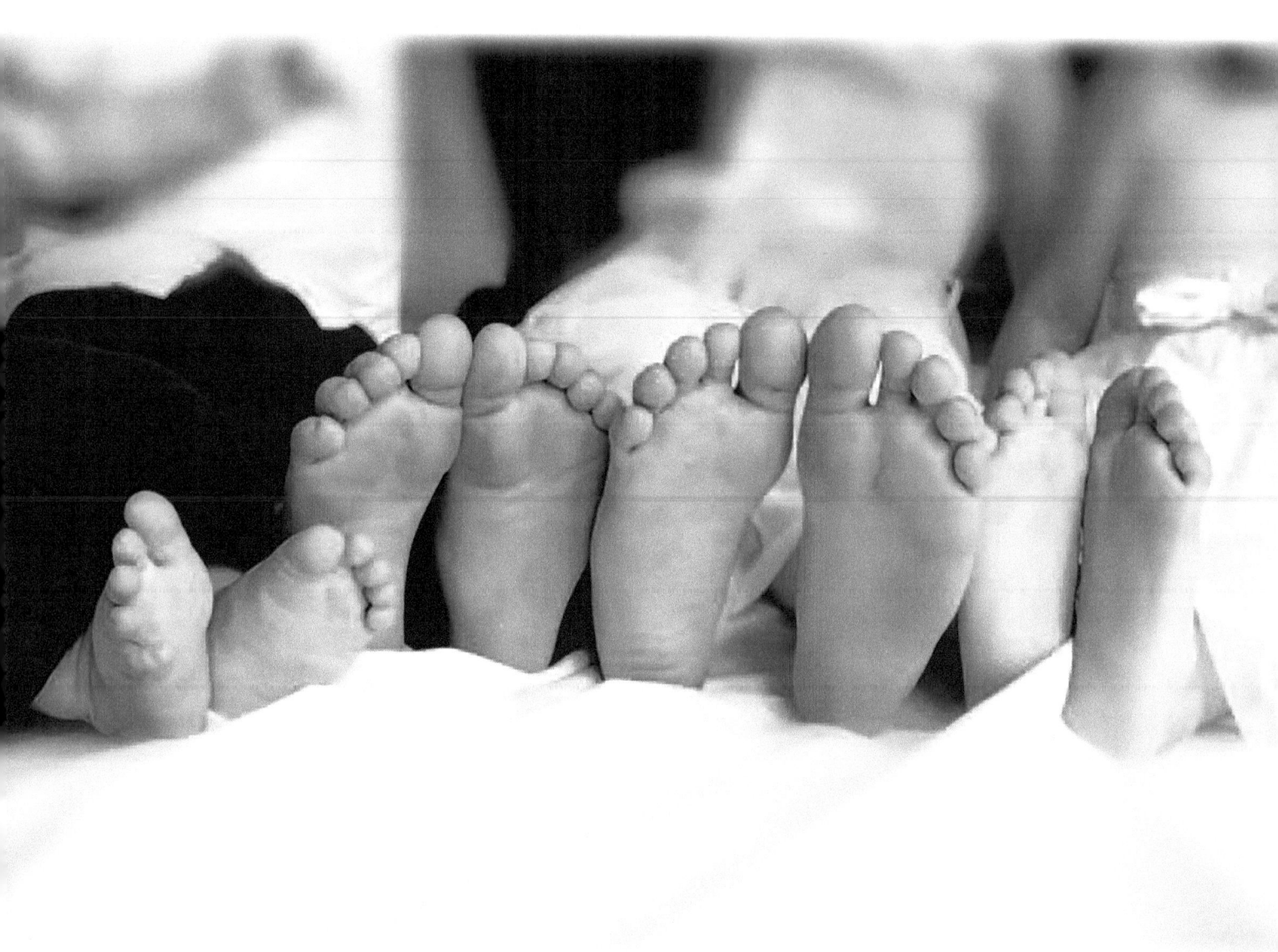

Memories

I rest in the reverie of my memories.
Though not in the distant past,
They awaken misty feelings of time lost to the ages.

Those fleeting days are the filmy pages
of warm and loving thoughts.
I turn them over in my mind and touch
the gilded edges of days gone by.

Those moments in time past bring me tears of sadness,
But smiles of remembrance, too.
My motherhood is captured in the volumes of my boys.

From a fiery hill, Sir Brendon came into view.
He was a beautiful child who stole my heart away.

Into a shelly valley I stepped to pluck up sweet Sir Sheldon.
His starry eyes ensnared my soul for all eternity.

Along the way my steps encountered Sir Landon.
His entry upon the land of life brought music to my soul.

While looking across the valley of my present joys,
Into my life came the still, deep presence of Sir Jordon.

A woman may be richly blessed by gifts of wealth and fame,
But my glory lies in those who came to join me in life.

Brendon, Sheldon, Landon, Jordon!
Gifts from God, I am more richly blessed than I could ever ask.

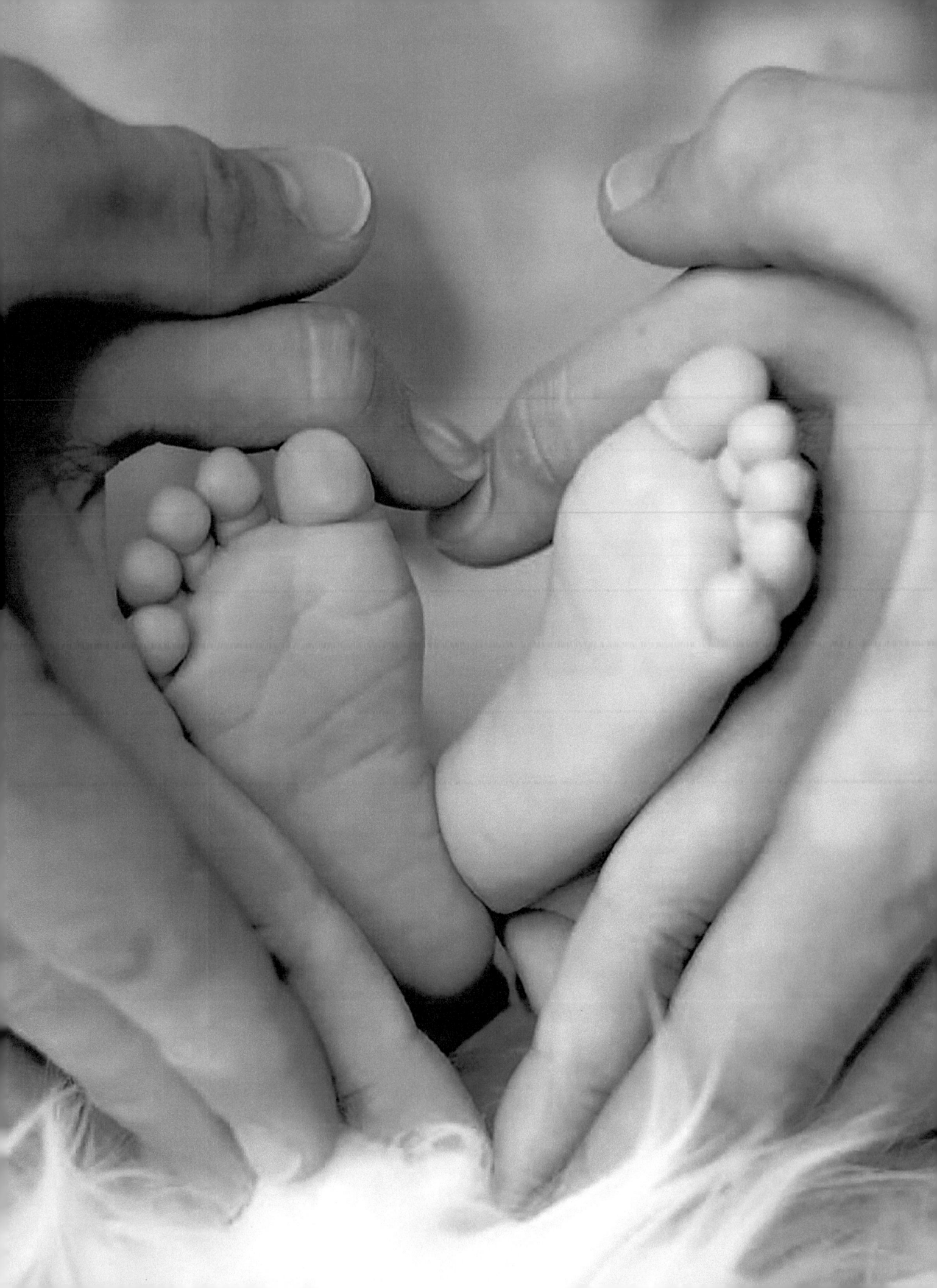

ON BECOMING A MAN

In my son's short life
He needed me to grow!

He and I were one.

For a moment in time
We were no longer one!

Mother and child were two.

Today you and I parted again.
Your bride and you were wed!

You and she became one.

For another moment in time
I stood beside her bed!

Mother and child became two.

Mothers and children become two
But for a short time are one!

Now you belong to another – my son!

SUMMER

May 8, 1997

The Flag

She waves at me as I pass by.
She makes me smile and think
Of all who've passed beneath her stripes
And stars so bright on field of blue.

She smiles at me with colors bright.
The crimson red of blood was shed;
The white's eternal life's reward.
How can we look without regard?

The years gone by since '76
Remind me time rushes on,
But patriots true follow her
To battlefields anew.

I do not understand
What draws them nigh?
It must be love indeed,
For freedom is not free!

The Patriot

He was a lad when he set out
A blond-haired, blue-eyed boy.
He knew not what lay 'round the bend
But duty called!

The call was not his chosen fate,
But what does a young man know?
His country called for him to go
And go he would!

Life's short day turned into night
As he approached the distant shore.
Defend the cause was all he knew
And that he did!

The days of light turned into hell
As cries of death defied them all.
His country's flag was there,
But that was all!

Wars will come as years go by;
It's the fate of freedom's call.
He lives those days e'en now,
E'er so long ago.

The blood and tears and cries for help
Fall upon the weak and brave,
But he recalls them all
For he answered duty's call.

The flag still flies, its colors bright!
Their blood—their faith—their purity
Remind us of his duty's call.
For that, we thank them all!

The Pelican

With beak thrust out
He dives beneath
The surface of the waves;
Then suddenly, he reappears
Before my wondering eyes.

Again, he soars with head held high
Above the sparkling shore;
And dives once more for silver fish
As I admire his sport.

This time he lands
Upon his feet and
Glides to a silent stop.
He gathers strength to launch again
While I await his flight.

Master diver
And pilot, too,
Show me once more your skills,
So that I might go home assured
That you dined well tonight.

The Sea

I **see** the sea
The sand and sea
Upon the glist'ning shore.

I **hear** the sea
The breaking sea
'Tis beck'ning to the shore.

I **smell** the sea
The briny sea
As gulls glide o'er the shore.

I **taste** the sea
The salty sea
On sun-kissed breezy shore.

I **touch** the sea
The sparkling sea
As diamonds on the shore.

I **sense** the sea
The boundless sea
The siren of the shore.

Three Sisters

On the sixteenth of June in forty-six
The first of the trio was born.
She was small and shy,
And a true Mama's baby – DEEDEE!

On the eighteenth of July in forty-seven
A second model appeared.
She had hair over her ears – a regular schmoo,
With eyes of blue like Daddy – GOGI!

On the twenty-second of September in forty-eight
Another young lady appeared.
Her entrance was joyful.
She was a bundle full of energy – SPARKPLUG!

The devoted father was delighted to report
All parts were present and accounted for.
And that was just alright
For he now had a bevy of four!

The young mother, though tired and worn,
Smiled down on each living doll.
She was delighted to see She now
was the mother of three!

Three little girls to care for – what a handful!
The oldest sported curly, blonde hair;
The second was tawny and straight;
The third was a strawberry blond.

Three little girls all dressed in pink;
What a delight for all eyes to see.
Are they triplets, people asked?
No, but they are so much alike.

As the little girls grew
It was easy to see
Each was as unique
As either of the others.

But the bond of their sisterhood
Brought them together
With kittens in a carriage
To motherhood!

The sand box beckoned on summer days
While mud pies baked in the brick oven.
Brown puddles rinsed dirty feet
And green pastures summoned young minds.

Chickens clucked,
Kittens snuggled,
Pigs oinked,
And birds sang.

Cows mooed,
Ducks waddled,
The dog barked,
And followed Daddy.

The garden beckoned willing hands:
Peas had to be plucked,
Beans needed to be boiled,
And the tomatoes stewed in their own juice.

Corn had to be cut from the cobs,
Cucumbers pickled in their brine,
Apples pureed, and
Pears packed in sugary syrup.

Carrots resembled little men in the nude,
Beets were burgundy orbs,
Meat was cooked tender, and
Cherries surrendered their pits.

The hundreds of jars lined the shelves:
Five hundred, or more,
Were packed by the labor of Mama's hands
To feed us all winter.

The kitchen was the heart of our home
Where bread baked, food simmered,
Lessons were learned,
And coffee was served each visitor.

The warming oven saved lives, too.
A piglet who lost his way found strength,
Kittens rescued from drowning were dried,
And nearly frozen feet were thawed.

Then the night came when we almost lost her;
The youngest was sick in the night.
The other two listened intently
Through the register overhead.

"It won't be long now, and we'll know
Which way it will go", the doctor said.
We feared for her life
And eavesdropped with baited breath.

She came around under the doctor's watchful gaze.
She was as thin as they come,
But a survivor, no less,
To serve as she was served.

She never knew what hit her
As she rounded the corner to the gate.
Daddy was coming
And she must make haste.

The blow was astounding
As her nose hit the pipe;
She reeled in pain,
Her small nose creased with blood.

Despite his best efforts
To quell her extreme fright
Daddy reckoned her injury was slight,
But it led to much more suffering.

The fear of cancer frightened her so
She buried the truth for ten years.
That Sunday the burden was so heavy
She broke down and wept openly.

Everything came out alright;
The lump was benign, but large.
It made her lopsided,
Yet able to nurse her babies.

The country school just around the corner
Was a hothouse of learning
With eager young minds
Soaking up the facts.

One became a secretary,
Another an artist,
The third a nurse—
All determined to be her own woman.

The school bell rings no more,
The flag has been folded,
And the door closed
To the ages past.

But learn, we did!
The best experiences we had
Were gleaned in that one-room school
Of yesteryear!

Cahill, Hartman, Nevels, and Love,
Mrs. Osborn was the best of all five.
We wrote stories, sang songs,
And read books every day.

The outhouse was privy to secret thoughts
And ponderings long past.
Snakes and spiders invaded our privy;
Oh, how it made us all cringe!

The piano is long gone,
The woods tell no tales,
The creek babbles on,
But the lessons are long silent.

Over the years we've moved along
From north to south and in-between.
But the best is yet to be,
For we sisters, three!

We come and go between homes
From a fair peninsula to the show-me and lone star states.
Though distance is great
Our hearts are united!

We will never forsake one another.
We are like the three little kittens
Who lost their mittens,
But we'll always come home to each other!

AUTUMN

CHAPTER 3

BY DARLENE T. EWERS

AUTUMN LEAVES

Autumn leaves are falling down
From lofty oak
And Stately maple tree.

I marvel at the various hues
Amid the conifers
And Sky so blue.

The contrast takes my breath away
As mountains shine with dew
While
Eagles soar.

Up and over the hills I drive
Following the ribbon roads
As
Clouds float by.

The sun shines brightly in the east
As I wend my way today
And
Deer graze.

I love this time of year
And all the vibrant hues
While
Birds sing.

I wish the leaves would stay awhile
But they fly away
As
The world turns cold.

AUTUMN   **September 28, 2008**

EMOTIONS

Once upon my mother's breast
I yearned for comfort and for rest.
From this world's darkness, cold and wrong,
I sought her arms—soft, warm, and strong.

But as I grew,
I finally knew
That she could not replace
The lonely feelings I would face.

Lord, as I've traveled through this plain,
I've often felt alone—in pain.
My mother's breast
Could give no rest.

It's in these times of deepest sorrow
I've learned to trust in my tomorrow.
Knowing now You bring me rest;
And loving You, You are my Guest.

AUTUMN   November 2, 19943

MY GUARDIAN ANGEL

Oh, would that I could, my guardian see!
A creature of God, my champion is he.
Softly and tenderly, please come unto me!
White as a cloud, yet bright as a star –
Stand near me now, Friend, and don't watch afar.

Though now I must walk through life's boundless sea,
God poured His goodness and love forth unto me.
He sent forth His maid, to plant and be free.
His servant comes now, her footsteps to keep.
No journey is too small or mountain too steep.

Someday life will halt, my journey will end.
My servant and I together shall wend
Onward together toward the valley's dark end.
My servant shall guard me and tend me with care
'Till my Savior I see and go home to live with Him there.

God spoke – and man was created.
Jesus spoke – and man was forgiven.
The Holy Spirt spoke – and man knew God.
Father, Son, and Holy Ghost – three in one - the Holy Trinity!

AUTUMN **January 11, 1984**

SUNFLOWERS

Sunflowers dancing in a field of sunshine remind me of your sunny face.

They pop up in the least expected place:

At the edge of fields of corn or framing a country garden.

Waiting and waving, standing tall and strong

They replace barrenness with their bright smiles.

If sunflowers beautify such a place with their quiet presence,

How much more the joy of your friendly face?

Your smile generates so much more than these sunny blooms.

It reminds me of your love and grace;

And alone, or not, it helps me stand firmly in my own garden.

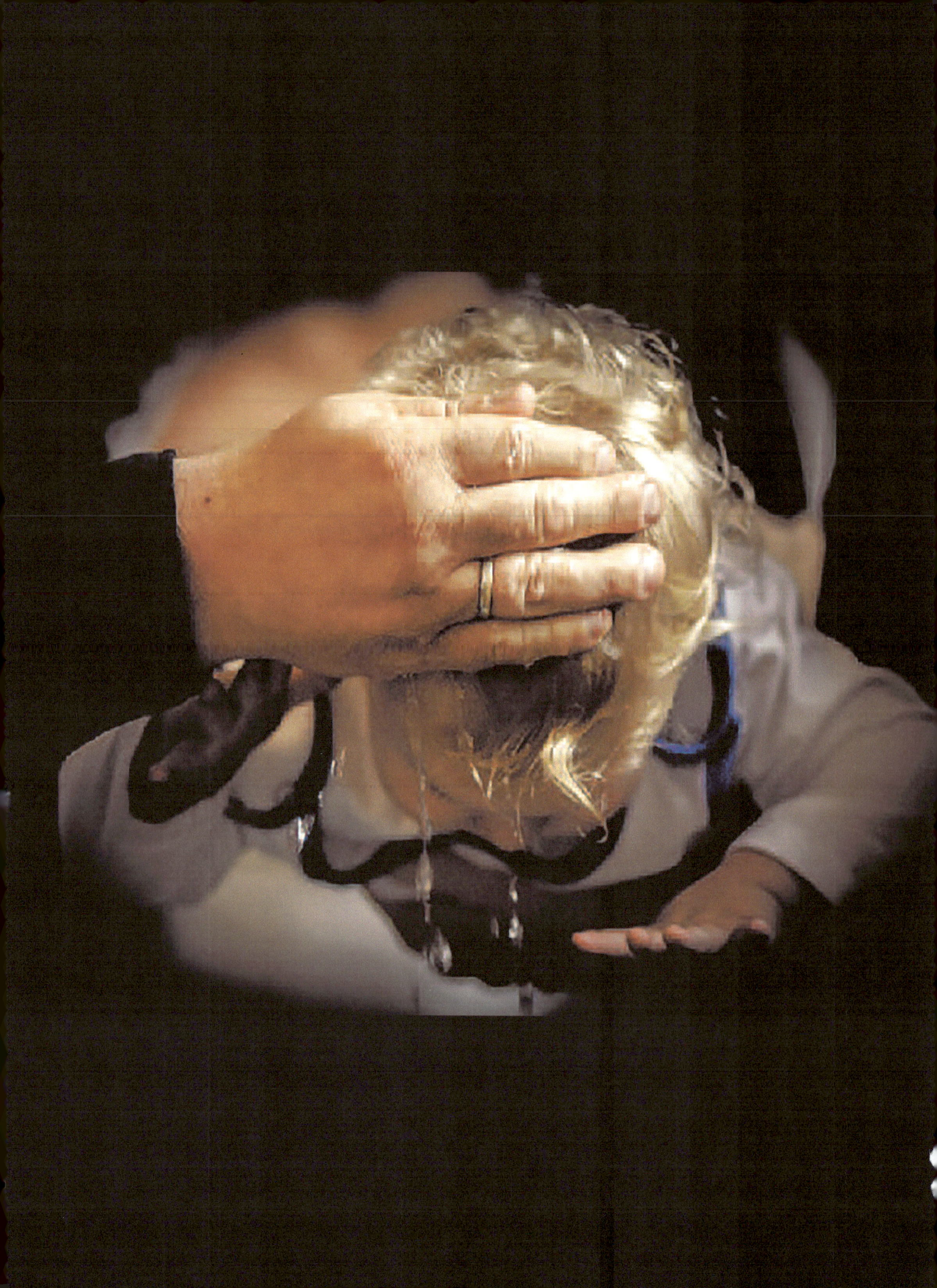

THANKFULNESS

Thank you, Lord, for cleansing me!

Holy Spirit, down you came!

Alpha and Omega, Thee!

Naught can tear me from Thy claim!

King eternal!

Father divine!

Unsurpassing grace sublime!

Love unfailing, endlessly.

Nearer now, I am to Thee.

Eternal life, Thy gift to me:

Sinner, Thine!

Savior, mine!

AUTUMN

January 11, 1994

THANKSGIVING DAY REMEMBERED

'Ere the morning sun arises, the turkey roasts in my oven—
It's such a delicious fragrance to enjoy.
Homemade pies await eager consumption on my sideboard—
Creamy pumpkin and luscious apple scents the room.
My hands combine the ingredients for the dressing—
Only Grandma's recipe will do!

Sounds of laughter erupt from the living room of my abode—
The television declares its sounds of joy.
My grown sons engage in the pleasure of childhood memories—
Sharing tales of their lives, while relaxing by the heartily roaring fire.
Their father muses at their stories wild—
And I relive them quietly, too!

The background revelry joins with a melodious sound to my ears—
My daughters-in-law are involved in their own social reveries.
I've been given the gift of daughters by my boys—
My bountiful life is a pleasure to behold.
Our grandchildren add their laughter, too—
How wonderful they are all here!

The potatoes are boiling in their pot, and I baste and prod the bird—
Hoping all turns out the way I'd planned so we can soon sit down to eat.
Relishes in red, green, and orange festoon the bowls—
And a casserole bakes in yonder room.
My cupboard has produced the bounty here—
And my heart is full!

"Time waits for no man", or so the poet says—
I've worked and fretted often, Lord, to prepare this spread;
But looking back, it seems so long ago that my boys were little ones—
How fast the ages run, and generations come and go.
I wish I could be young again, but then—
I'd miss today!

AUTUMN   November 17, 2012

The Harp

Lying silently beneath my hands,
The strings await my touch.
I pause to find the notes,
Then gracefully arch my hands.
My fingers find their mark
And gently pluck the strings.

The sounds of angels' songs
Come sweetly flowing forth.
The notes float up toward heaven
As God's Spirit inspires my heart.
My soul rises heavenward
As angels seem to sing!

I may a mortal be
But my soul has risen
To the place where angels live.
For when you hear their song
Upon my harp so grand
You've heard the praise of God!

The Sweater

I do not know how old it is or when it came to be,
But the label states:
Macys * 100% Polyester
Made in Korea WP = 8046.

The young woman worked for room and board,
Then sent the rest to Mama.
There were children to clothe
And she had no need.

I do not know whether she bought it in the Mile-high city,
Or downtown KCMO.
She was young and working hard,
So why not buy a sweater?

Though plain in style, the memories take me back
To those distant days on the farm.
She wore it then
And now I wear it, too.

The old beige sweater warmed her back as she went to fetch the water.
It accompanied her to the chicken coup
To gather eggs or fowl
While the garden grew our supper.

And in the cool of morning, while preparing our food,
Or tending to her girls,
She often produced a hanky
From the pocket in her sweater.

When her husband called to ask a hand, she helped him cut the wood.
She took the time to feed the chicks,
To bring a calf into the world,
And carry in the wood.

Ages have passed me by, but memories of the farm
Come back to warm my heart.
When I put her sweater on,
Memories linger near.

The cows are gone, the chickens, too, and butchering days are done.
The jars of produce are no more,
But memories come to me
When I put her sweater on.

I know not when it comes to be that I wear a radiant robe;
For now, her sweater covers me.
It served her well through all those years,
But now it covers me.

The Trinity

Dear Lord,   I see Thee in the risen Son,
　　　　　　　I see Thee in the setting sun.

Dear Father,   I see Thy hand upon the mirror lake
　　　　　　　And majestic mountain peak.

My Jesus,   I see Thy love reflected
　　　　　　　In the beauty of a child.

Holy Spirit,   I feel Thy presence
　　　　　　　Upon the rustling wind.

　　　　　　　And if I look within myself,
　　　　　　　I see Thee there as well.

AUTUMN　　　　　　　　　　　　　　　　**October 16, 1983**

The Window of My World

My first view of the world was at my birth
And what an experience that was for Mama and me!
But I entered life undaunted and ready to take it on,
Although It was just the first of how cold the world can be.

After nearly three-quarters of a century
I've experienced various and a myriad of things.
These have educated me to what really matters
And the true value of human beings.

Being guided by the beliefs and opinions of my parents
Was just the beginning of what my guidelines would be.
Grade school added flavor to my experiences
But high school was a shock to such a shy one as me.

College enriched my values and beliefs
And confirmed by my faith, defined my life's purpose.
God revealed His call to me there
And that was the beginning of my adventures.

My assignment sent me out into the wider world
Where I met more Christians than ever before.
The defining moment was when I met my husband
And that solidified my future.

Our marriage led to thirteen moves and four sons,
who in turn, enriched my life and womanhood.
To this day, I marvel at what I've learned from them
And the difficulties each one has withstood.

Those boys have given us daughters, grandchildren, and more.
They say that a generation is forty years, and I'm approaching two.
With one more year to go, we will celebrate our golden years
By bringing our family together for a big to-do.

What the future brings into our lives, we do not know,
But as I look out my window, east or west, north or south,
I cannot see the world beyond, but I know it isn't here.
My future is yet to come, and it's above!

God grant me the grace to reach beyond this horizon and
By the grace of Christ, who died and rose again for me, I'll live!

AUTUMN   **October 17, 2017**

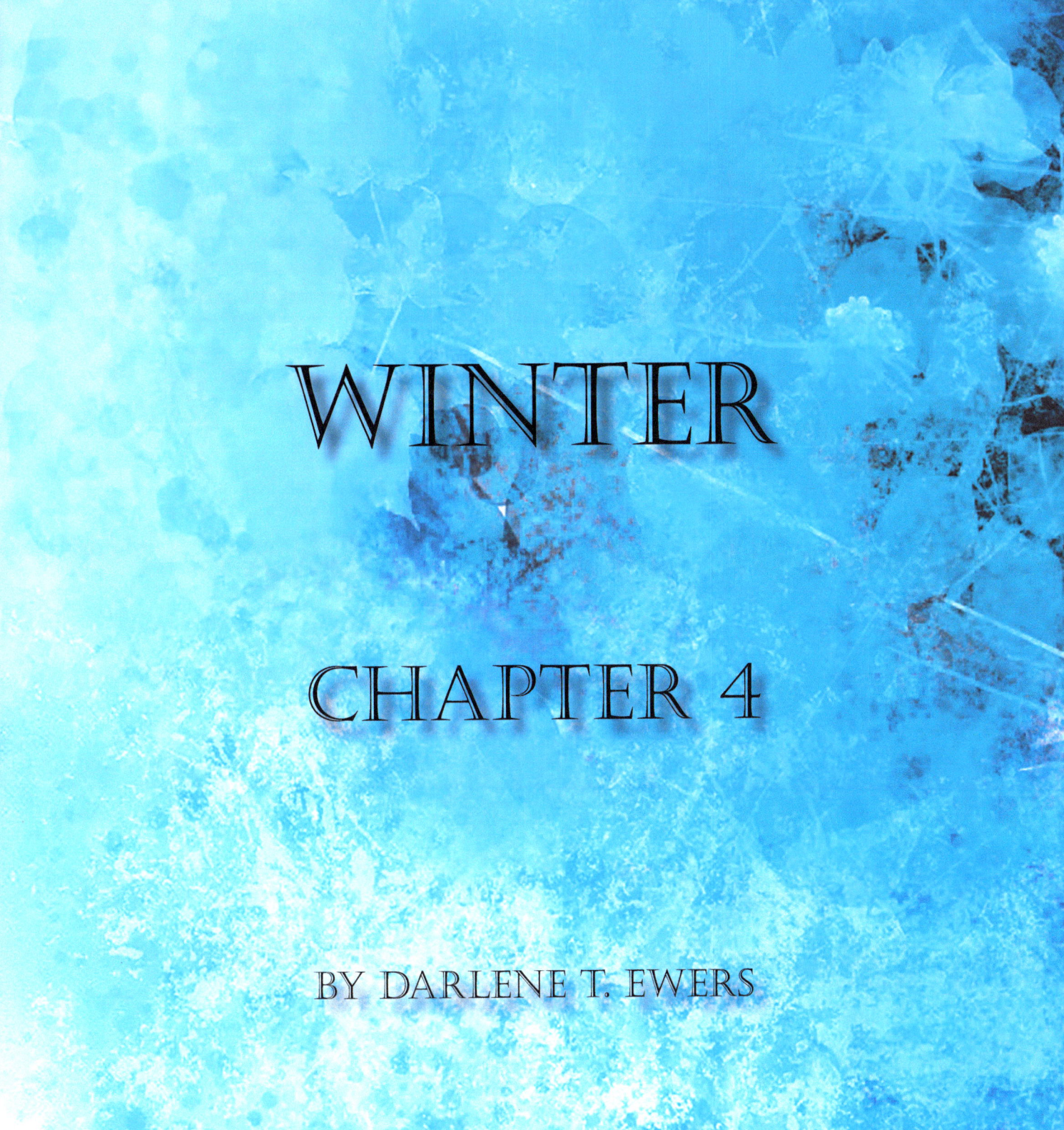

WINTER

CHAPTER 4

BY DARLENE T. EWERS

CHRISTMAS MEMORIES

Crackling kindling and burning wood in our fireplace contributes to the scent of festive winter activities.

Hot kitchen ovens embellish the homey scene with the fragrant smells of spices baking in cakes, cookies, and pies.

Red cranberries and fluffy white popcorn festoon the green boughs waiting to serve a buffet to our feathered friends.

Icing on crisp sugar cookies remind us of the toys we received and the Christmas decorations in our home.

Sparkling white crunchy snow appears to have glitter sprinkled across its shiny surface.

The pine tree standing in the family living room emits the fresh clean smell of dark green forests.

The Christ Child welcomes our celebration of His precious birth!

GRACE

I awoke this morning to a blanket of white fleece
    covering the valley.
Lacey white flakes trickled silently toward
    sleeping earth's face.
All of nature lay there, gently
sleeping under her fallen grace,
    Yet I could not help
pondering the meaning of God's carefree folly.

We awaken to the duties of each day,
while God plods along through the ages,
Waiting patiently for each of us
    to awaken to the meaning of it all.
Why did Adam and Eve give in to Satan's lies,
    losing their peace in the fall?
He awaits our choice – you and I –
    as our battle with Satan rages.

Sleep on dead earth under fleecy pall.
    God's grace awaits us all.

WINTER   **March 7, 2007**

Grandma's Sugar Cookies

Snowflakes fall while angels sing:
"Glory to the newborn King!"
Bright yellow stars and the half-moons glow
While miniature trees lie in a row.

Little Santas are dressed in reds
Lying beside snow-white sleds.
While little wreaths get candied tarts,
The fluffy rabbits tug at hearts!

Crisp, white rounds and flowers trite
Sparkle in the sullen light.
Each small form tells the story
Of God's hope born in glory!

Grandma's recipe now is mine!
Her crisp, light cookies share our time
And that's why they have come to be
Part of our Christmas reverie!

HAPPY
<u>A</u> long time ago a baby was born in Bethlehem.
<u>P</u>rophets foretold his coming as our Savior and a
<u>P</u>ious man named Simeon proclaimed Him!
<u>Y</u>eshua has arrived and is our Messiah!

BIRTHDAY
<u>I</u>n the stable, animals bent over his cradle!
<u>R</u>egal angels announced his lowly birth!
<u>T</u>he shepherds bowed humbly before him!
<u>H</u>is mother pondered all these things. A
<u>D</u>onkey bore her to the stall so lowly!
<u>A</u>nd Joseph stood afar wondering!
<u>Y</u>eshua has arrived and is my son!

JESUS!
<u>E</u>verlasting Father!
<u>S</u>avior of the world!
<u>U</u>nited with the Spirit!
<u>S</u>on of God!

MAY GOD BLESS YOUR CELEBRATION OF HIS COMING!

WINTER **December 24, 2009**

SEASONS AND SENSES

Brush strokes of Thy hand brand new;
Velvet grass all green and blue;
Rustling leaves of tender youth;
Damp new scent of violet hue;
I stretch my arms to reach the sky
And greet Thy Spirit from on high!

Crimson roses blush with dew;
Musky grass and rainbows new;
Songbirds sing upon their perch;
Velvet blossoms like a torch;
Melon nectar dripping, cool;
Jesus' sweetness is God's own tool!

Amber straw and rusty earth;
Corn on stalks and pumpkin's girth;
Crisp blue mornings, fog's soft shawl;
Apples crunch and winds do howl;
Father, mine, Thy hand hast blest my life;
And on it Thy smile does rest.

Whiteness bright and frozen earth;
Ice hangs on with frost and mirth;
Azure blue of sky and lake;
Warmth of hearth and home alike;
Father, Son, and Spirit shine!
Thee alone — I claim Thee mine.

WINTER

January 11, 1984

Sisters

As winter passes steadily by
I ponder each fresh day anew.
While sitting before a hearthside fire,
I think of larks, blue skies, and you.

My heart is not a cold, hard stone,
Because it's full of love for you.
Memories bring thoughts of long ago,
And scenes of times with you.

They sparkle in the sunlight,
Like drops of morning dew.
My heart feels warm though growing old,
Because of love for you.

Springtime, too, has passed me by,
And Summer's glow of youth.
Fall winds blow now upon my brow
Like gentle thoughts of you.

If only life were not so short
I'd have more time to do
The things I want and love to share
With sisters sweet as you.

Gentle skies and love so true
Will always be my wish for you.
My lasting prayer shall always be,
Love, joy, and peace eternally!

THE GIVING TREE

There's a golden glow in the winter sky,
Which the morning light exudes.
It sparkles on the glittering dawn
As snowflakes trickle down.

I catch a glimpse of fluttering wings
Gliding by my window pane.
The chickadees are flying in
To dine on seeds and grain.

Amidst the blue jays' chatter, none too soon,
Come the squirrels and doves.
They anxiously peruse the seeds
That fall beneath the pine.

I sip upon a cup of brew and
Marvel every morn.
Not a single day goes by, anon,
But they entertain me, too!

The morning light dissolves into
A brighter tone by noon.
I check again to see what crowd
Has gathered 'round my pine.

To my surprise, a herd of deer
Have gathered about to feed.
Behold, there's not just one below,
But five beneath my tree!

Look now! My love, the wonder I behold
That spreads beneath my tree.
The does begin to snort and shove –
Those greedy, gray-haired dames!

And then up glides the mother deer
With twins against her side.
She scatters the brood assembled there
And lets her babies feed.

I marvel at the scene of life
Beneath my small green pine.
The Good Lord tends them by my hand
Around the snow-crowned tree.

As daylight's sun turns into dusk,
he snowflakes flutter down.
The golden glow casts one last beam
On bird and bough and bye'.

I look again through window pane
At trampled snow aground,
And thank my God for all he gives
To me and those below.

The sky is dark, the sun is gone,
And now my tree stands free.
The chirps and chatters, snorts and grunts
Are silent now to me.

The sparkling stars come out to dance,
The moon to light their way.
The angels sing up in the sky
And smile upon my tree.

I will sleep till morning's light
Shines down on us anew.
I cannot wait to take delight
In the creatures gathered there.

As midnight's shade gives way to dawn
A small grey hare hops into view.
His ears perk up to distant sounds
As he nibbles on the apple there.

The feast's begun anew!

The Three Little Girls

The three little girls
Have lost their curls
And won't try to find them.
They chose to leave home,
Ne'er to return,
Leaving the past behind them.

The three young women
Went out to find men,
But didn't know whence they would come.
Their choices were made
And plans that were laid
Came back now and then to haunt them.

The three older ladies
Have lost their thin middles
But never fear or regret them.
We each have a home
And children who warm them;
The future is bright on our shores.

The time for tears
May leave its marks;
Regrets are few and far behind them.
But we all trudge on
And leave our kisses
On the cheeks of those that we cherish.

The children have gone
To make homes of their own,
And added a few to their own nests.
We hug them and kiss them
Then send them back home
Only to regret that we miss them!

WINTER

February 18, 2014

Time

Time exists in the physical world,
but it has no material elements.

It is invisible,
but its affects are seen.

It has no scent,
but it seasons life's memories.

It moves through the ages,
but occupies no space.

It changes people's lives,
but remains the same itself.

It has no sound,
except when we celebrate!

WINTER WONDERLAND

Whipped cream on pine trees,
Vanilla ice-cream along the highway,
Blue skies for a cover,
And bright sunlight are my sunlamp!

People enjoy one another
As they ski, skate, and slide down hills.
Children build memories
And dogs join in the fun.

Moms make hot mugs of chocolate,
Children build snow forts,
Dads bring in the lumber,
And start a warming fire.

People complain as they get old,
But what is the reason?
Don't they enjoy creamsicles
Or frosted sundaes in the summer?

I think God is just showing us
That He likes them, too.
When He sends snow dancing
In driveways and across chimney tops!

God knows why He made seasons
So that we would wonder
Why the days grow shorter in winter
And longer in the spring.

Maybe He knows we need time to relax,
To read a good story,
To sip on a frothy hot mug,
Or to snuggle in front of a fire.

"Time waits for no man",
Or so the poet said.

But I choose to be content
And thank God for my cozy day.

A brief respite from the busy days
Of yesteryear carry me forward
Into the 'morrow as I contemplate
Memories during my reverie.

I don't know why I am able to tolerate
The frozen winter days like
Some enjoy the heat of summer.
I choose to be mellow today.

I have comfort knowing
That as my clock winds down,
Tonight, or over the years,
I choose to find solace in the silence.

The robins will return,
The squirrels, too.
Nesting mourning doves
Will soon coo.

Fish will soon travel upstream
To mate and to spawn.
Kittens, and puppies, and calves
Will be born.

The crops will be harvested
And pumpkins reach full girth,
Hay will be stacked,
And harvests brought home.

After all of earth brings forth her own,
The time will come for the earth to surrender
To the silence of winter,
And the solace of the winter wonderland!

WINTER   **January 19, 2016**